Of Fear and Love

How then, would you choo
Harbored behind walls of fearful history,
a castle built to protect, your sanctuary
of slow starvation, a place to be safe,

yet alone, waving from the castle walls,
a thing of beauty seen, but never touched,
slowly hardening to an exquisite perfection,
wondered at as you waste to bones?

Or would you die spectacularly,
leaping from the walls, daring gravity,
full of faith that feeds you, Love
that caresses your soul and skin,

and lifts you above the battle
to spectacular victory or defeat,
feeling each arrow, sling and yet
unconquerable, a soul of myth come to life?

I know my choice,
and it is a fearful one, yet
I will expose my heart, soft
and beautifully vulnerable,

and dare the world
to make it hard.

Therapy

There is that moment, when you decide to enter
the dark places, the hallways you kept locked
for so long in hopes that the ghosts would be satisfied.

But they never are.

No, ghosts are voracious.
they feed on fear and silence,
feast on being kept in the night,

and die only in the sun.

Removing

And when you shed
every lie you dressed in for others,
every inhibition you hid in fear,
every insecurity they chained you with,

then, and only then,
will your beauty shine
and you will find what I already know,
that you are irresistible
beyond words.

Things in the Mirror

Somehow, when you look back,
it all looks so distant,
historical, a thing pressed neatly
into a book, all wrapped up

and having none of the messiness
of real life, luring you
into a sense of false security,
as if the past had no power

until, like a ghost with claws,
it climbs out of it's coffin
to remind you that some things never die,
they are only caged.

The Poet's Truth

This is the truth:
Too often I feel like a cripple,
unable to find the words
to express the depths
of my passion, my fears, my struggle.

All my study and practice,
all my years toiling at my craft
feel wasted, shallow, a cosmic tease
to fill a heart with so much,
then lock it all in with a lack of language,

trying, always trying
to capture the essence
before it flies away,
life's vibrant colors laughing
at the cripple who dares to dance.

Locks

You come around the corner
and there it is, the chain
slightly rusted, it's heavy links still strong
and vigorous, guardians

of some secret hidden
behind walls and gates,
something precious perhaps,
or dangerous beyond words,

a dream captured long ago
and held prisoner, held for ransom,
leaving you to wonder
if what lies behind is friend or foe.

The lock is strong, blemished by scars
a thing of terrible efficiency,
determined to do its duty,
to remind those who are foolhardy

enough to believe in the treasure beyond
that others have tried and failed,
that the lock still stands
long after the suitors have left

shaking their heads in futility.
Some treasures, they say,
are easier to find than this
locked behind it's stone walls

and iron chains.
But you are no knight,
more the fool than hero,
a cat like creature, full of curiosity

without the sense to see defeat
when it stares you in the eye,
not even
when it takes the form of an eternal lock, and so

you reach your fearful arms and climb,
ignoring the carefully constructed walls
and fearful chains, climbing
like some blind Romeo

to the top of the ancient wall, and over
unsure whether it holds
a beautiful damsel, a rotting corpse,
or a dragon, hungry to be fed.

Unable

It's not quite bad enough,
not quite what they would call
a crisis, a breakdown.

You function
and the muscles around your smile
still work, perhaps

more out of habit than emotion,
but well enough
that passersby would never know

your fragility.
You dance in the night,
swaying alone to the Basin Street Blues,

music filling the room,
animating your struggling soul.
There should be bourbon

and a film noir blonde.
There should be smoke in the room,
an atmosphere of mystery

and falseness where even truth
is distrusted.
There should be the hero,

you, of course,
strong and certain, brash and brave,
never long the captive.

If nothing else, you have that right,
a refusal to die in chains,
fighting past the dark demons of your soul,

battered, scarred and swaying,
but still standing, fearful
but ready for the next fight,

unable to win,
unable to surrender.

The Fearful Cup

At this point in life,
there are no surprises.
You know what poison

lies await in each cup
that you have already tasted
time and again. You know

the agonies of those familiar draughts.
And you may choose them again,
the familiar demons,

safe in their pain,
or you may reach
for the fearful cup,

the one untasted,
and risk
the possibility

of joy.

The Child Part

Come. Rest.
Let the tears flow.
Tell stories.
Listen,

not to the crowds in your mind,
but to the quiet of your heart.

Truth lies there,
quiet,
simple.
The child part,

tempered with age
is stronger than you know.

After the Meal

Ah, those webs,
so thin, so weak,
barely there, seen only when the light
is just right,

living best in darkness,
those tiny contradictions
of softness and imprisoning strength:
the need, always the need

for strength, always; and for
vulnerability as long as it is
convenient and impeccably
timed,

all the pieces in place, like
a puzzle that has no place
for a piece missing,

where one must be perfection,
or else accused of honest weakness, or worse,
tossed to the waste bin

like a dead fish,
smelly, and wildly inappropriate
after the meal.

The Devil's Garden

It is too dark.
The path has wound too long.
It is dark, twisted,
the stuff of nightmares

that never wake.
The undergrowth is black-green
and creeps, almost alive,
reaches for you

in the moments you dare hope.
You are afraid.
You are lost, hungry
for the briefest wisp of sunlight.

You have fought ghosts,
fought indifference, fought
the hungry November fog
and now,

you are weary, ready
almost,
to lie down and let the creeping vines
draw you into their arms,

ready to surrender,
a task that should be easy,
just cease, and rest.
What a joy it would be to rest!

You shut your eyes.
You pray an uncertain prayer,
trusting God will know
what you do not,

that he will love you,
even in your brokenness,
whether you lay here for a black eternity
in the devil's garden,

or rise.
You listen to the silence, and,
bone weary,
you stand,

and walk.

The Trenches

This is where life is fought,
not on the parade ground with colors bright
and creases pin-sharp
create oohs and ahs from the spectators,
lined to watch the show,

Not in the battlefield
where bravery is expected
and reactions, not our minds
rule the day,

but here, in the dark holes
of the trenches,
where, helpless, our walls
protect us, and we hunker down,

preparing in silence
for that moment
where we charge,
or flee.

Every Death Has a Story

The building stands like a boxer, punch drunk,
a fresh coat of paint on the front,
the back and foundations battered,
abandoned,
the slow erosion of time and neglect leaving
a facade, waiting for the final beam to crack
or for the wrecker's ball to strike
one final blow,
to end the song, silence the music
that once lifted the hearts, like you,
now worn, now waiting,
a fraction, nay
less than that, of who and what you were,
still savable, but failing, struggling,
unwilling to collapse,
unable to rise,
echoes of opera and burlesque,
of soul dancing and moments of frivolous courage,
all resound in the silence,
you look at the whitewashed walls,
aware
that every death has a story,
even before it comes.

Art and Love

Sometimes it doesn't matter
if it makes sense or not.
It is enough
that it brings color and joy.

Two Ways to Maintain a Fence

You may paint it
each season,
and keep your vigilance,
replacing each slat
as they begin
to falter,
so you are sure
the wall never fails,
and you are protected,
always safe
and alone,
always behind
the perfect picket
so all will see you
and say
how beautiful your fence
is,
missing
what lies behind.

Or you may let it go,
refuse to repaint
or rebuild,
let it weaken
in seasons of summer storms,
let it lean,
break,
rot,
and slowly
have it fall
apart
so animals,
children,
and lovers
may push it over
and walk in.

A Glorious Madness

Perhaps then, I am mad.
I see color where there is none,
hear songs where only the wind blows,
feel passion in a single touch,

I believe in God and love and hope
where there is no evidence,
not even a scrap,
my heart leaps like a rabid fire.

Colors are brighter to me than cameras can capture,
and the songstress on the corner sings opera,
but only, only
to me.

I see art…… where no artist has been.
History, despite the evidence,
is painted with a watercolor wash,
soft and pastel, ignoring the blood
that washed down the cobblestones,

and disappears with the rain.
I see love, where most see only death,
and the threat of death.

My feet dance in the summer moonlight,
high atop the quarry. my lips still thrill
at a single kiss,
flushed as a schoolboy.

And I mourn in beauty,
remembering, always remembering
that which was there, that which was imagined,
and that which was never spoken.

Perhaps then, I am mad.
a glorious madness, full of beauty

and fire that keeps me awake at night,
simply remembering,

remembering,
too much, far too much
for one mind to hold,
so much it spills out
in a madman's lilting words,

in paint and photographs
of what is almost, almost
there.

The Glass
The glass is old,
so old it wrinkles the light,
transforming the sun lit landscape
into a Monet,

not quite real
a counterpoint
to the dark room
where you have sat quietly for so long,

the rippled sunlight
a tease,
a promise
held at bay,

framed like a museum piece.
You are unsure
precisely what lies on the other side,
but

you are certain of one thing:
There is light,

and the dark that has surrounded you,
crippled you,
held you at bay,

is one step closer to finishing
your long, slow murder.
Your fingers touch the glass,
so warm with hope
it brings tears to your eyes,

dripping memories that silently
fall
down your cheeks.

"Enough!" your heart cries,
as your hand grasps the stone and raises it,
refusing to be a prisoner any longer,
refusing to live in a house without doors,
determined to find the light,

unconcerned whether the details will look the same
when the glass is shattered,
unconcerned that the shards may
cut you, that your own blood may be shed,

the bright red mingling,
painful and real as the landscape almost in sight,
sure

that the light, real, warm and enveloping
is better

than this safe, dark corner
where you have lived
so long.

Every New Death
I have seen it
before,
the slow decay,
the rot,
so plainly visible,
as neglect,
slowly stripped
the color,
stripped
the strength
from the carefully constructed
love,
and left it raw
to the weather,
slowly strangled,
bereft
of the strength
to color itself
alive,
simply waiting for death
while everyone
watches,
beautifully blind,
somehow sure
the ending
will not be
what every new death
promises,
always surprised
when
the end arrives
with a crash,
forgetting,
always forgetting
they have watched it
day,
by day,
by day.

Intimacy

This is what I had hoped for
but never expected,
the same color
but with texture so different
it feels new.

Danger of Floods

As the storm approaches
you head for higher ground,
clambering up rocks already slick
with the damp drizzle that has begun to fall.
You climb, aware of the danger of floods
that have more than once carried you
like a rag doll, down the river
and left you broken. You bones still ache
at the memory.

And so you climb, cut and bruised,
for the lone tree that still stands
true as the cross on Calvary,
a survivor and a beacon both,
not so much from the storm itself
which will rage through the night,
but from being swept away
to a place where your body and soul
will never be found.

The Real Work

The real work
is not to build the wall.

No, that is easy,
a natural progression

of fear and hurt.
The real work is to tear it down,

brick by brick
and let the barbarians and lovers in.

Cherries

On the stairs outside a few errant cherries fall,
lipstick perfect, the color of a lover's lips,
not gaudy, but rich with desire and promise,
tender, soft, so perfect

you cannot resist a taste.

Still Waters

The day will come
when the storms pass,

and your head falls still
and you remember love

without fear.

Hard Love

Don't tell me love is soft.
True love is hard,
full of pain and disappointment,
not for sissies or the easily frightened,
full of twists and turns,
and requires superhuman faith
in something invisible as the wind,
belief
that this thing that has broken your heart
again and again
is not malevolent and mad,
but knows better than you
what is important for your soul to hear.

Only then, is seems,
when you succumb to the madness
and give yourself to it
like a child in a thunderstorm
full of fear and wonder in equal amounts,
only then

does it come to rest,
does it become soft,
does it come
to stay.

Man as Modern Art

Excuse me
as I flounder through my feelings,
unequipped to see through sandstorms
of emotions flying,
seeking a place to hide
before I am overwhelmed,

Seeking
a path, a way to make sense
of the love and hate, passion and fear
and their diabolical dance.

No one told me.
It was not part of my education.
In fact, they were suspect,
things of no value.

Life was simple.
Be a man
meant never crying,
a stoic face that never cracked.
You were this.
or that.
Never both.

No one told me
life was a constant battle
of heart and head, of emotions
battling in the same soul
like a cage fight
where no one ever dies
and the fighting never stops.

Which is why I stop.
I let the dust settle.
I let the storm pass
as I stand in the rain, arms outstretched.
Still.

I wish,
every day I wish
to be the simple man.
All this.
All that.
Sure.

Instead I am a madman's canvas,
splattered and smeared
with colors that do not belong with each other,
and yet, somehow
they do.

Casualty of Love.
Yes,
I believe in love
even
when i cannot see it, even
when it fails me,
even
in those moments when it is ripped
out of my chest — a casualty of wars
that are not my own.

I believe in love,
not because I am wise in it,
for I have never been wise, it seems.
I love stupidly
like a child,
too innocently to be trusted
with anything
as precious as love.

So let me wrap my wounds
before they fester,
before they turn dark and fatal.
Let me pour the salve of God on them
and hope he understands
the all too human frailty
of someone so simple
that he insists
on believing in love.

Sit

Come and sit a while,
here on this old bench.
Talk to me, or not.
Be content

to simply feel the warmth
of the afternoon sun,
the comforting presence

of each other.

Perilous Thoughts

Yes, perhaps I am a bit insane.
I confess it now to release you
from any apprehension
that I may need to be listened to,
that there is wisdom in my fool's words,

that there is reason to believe in love
in the midst of pain, even if
it is the pain that reminds me
how powerfully love burrows into our soul
and refuses to release us

even after death.
Laugh at me when I believe it can strike
in a moment, that it surrounds us
in beauty and light, in flowers and lambs
as much as the tenderest caress in the night.

And if I, Quixote-like, love whores and ladies,
children and ancient ruins with the same
slightly offbeat ardor;

well then, that is that is my particular madness
and I claim it, holding it close,

preaching, holding that love to my breast
like a snake handler,
well aware love has the power
to raise a man from the dead,
or kill him in his finest moment.

All About the Unknown

Life is a series of scars,
each more painful and more beautiful
than the last,
a lattice work of wounds

from wars you were often unaware
you were fighting,
the mystery solved only after
your corpse was found,

beautifully battered,
and not yet dead.
at least,
on the outside.

Preachers and medicine men dance
and chant, their songs swing wildly
between dirge and dance,
incantations of belief in life after life,

life after wounds, life
after the little death that plagues us all,
dark and seepingly
colorful endings, deserving of a Fellini film.

This is what they know:
there is no death.
There is only change,
a bloody kaleidoscope

wild with the tiny flakes of color,
yours and others you know and
do not recognize,
all dancing like those afflicted

by love.

Dancing With Storms

You always seem so still,
stoic, strong,
an ancient house on the hill,
always there through the storms,

but the truth is,
like an ancient house you were built to move,
to shift in the wind,
the pegs that hold the strong beams
fit lightly, run deep,
and creak in the wind.

That creaking is the sound of your strength,
movement made audible,
no pretense at perfection,
it is your imperfection, and its acceptance,
even the design for it
that helps you stand against the angriest wind.

No, storms will not take you down.
Erosion. Rot. Neglect.
Those are the enemy.

Slow. Invisible day to day,
only they can render you dead or dying.

And so you breath. You write your life,
Scanning for the weakness of rot,
the soft death of neglect
refusing to die that slow death,
preferring to stand, creaking and moving,
always moving,
dancing,
with storms.

The Heart's Butterflies

They rise unexpectedly,
even from the dead,
a flittering excitement,
half fear, half hope,
anticipation
that cannot be predicted
or protected,
only savored
in its glorious vulnerability.

Beyond Your Reach

There is light there.
You can see it,
just beyond your reach,
through a dark,
unlistening place,
a gentle black hole
that loves and drains your lifeblood
in equal measure,
or maybe in uneven measure,
gently hungry,
leaving you

fragile,
more broken than you appear,
but still, step by timid step
you walk,
the walking wounded,
you walk.

There is light there.
and it is not beyond your reach.

Lost

Words,
your armor and sword,
your unraveler of mysteries,
your lover's caress,
your comforter and soapbox
are suddenly empty,
stripped of power,

leaving you

lost

like the child
you always were,
and always will be,
crying, crying
for a mother's touch.

Tombstones

When I am gone,
bury me deep
and paint my tombstone
red,

the color of passion,
jarring perhaps,
unsettling in a place
where decorum is the rule,
but truer than a name
and a date,
let color shout my love,
inappropriately vibrant,
so powerful
it should never be allowed
to die.

Why I Cling to You in the Night.

The children were right.
There are monsters in the dark,
mad demons we create ourselves

and try desperately to hide,
to stuff in the back closet
and under the bed,

monsters we embellish
with every fear we can conjure.
We feed them in the night,

sure they are growing,
but unsure how large, or
how voracious they are becoming

in the black of night.
Our only saviors
are God and lovers,

the ones who stay with you,
breath of their love the only sound
in the night.

So yes, I cling to you in the dark.
I gain power from the warmth of your soft skin.
Power to survive the night

Power to know
that the creatures I created,
I can kill.

Lion in the Garden

As you eat your eggs and bacon,
the cup of coffee steaming;
As you nibble on the toast,
smeared thick with orange marmalade;

As you contemplate the night before,
and the days, months, years behind you,
you are aware
of how badly you share

the things that matter the most.
Not from lack of trying.
No, not that.

Your words have filled the air,
filled page after page,
hour after hour, late into the night,

disappearing like fog in the morning,
under the bright sun of other's imaginings and pasts.

You sip your coffee, strong,
slightly bitter, slightly sweet,
and wonder, as you have wondered so often,
What if?

What if those you loved felt that love?
What if they knew
the depth, the rawness, the fear......
the passion

those three words meant?
What if they knew the trueness, how
even with the flaws and mistakes,
the misstarts and madness,

you are crazy true,
unwavering, that your desire
despite the grey hair and rheumy eyes
still burns?

You sigh.
No one would believe.
No one ever has.
You are too quiet perhaps,
your words lack the force.

You do not shout.
You simply say.
and that, it seems
is never enough.

Scars

Let me kiss your scars,
linger over them with my lips and love,
celebrate them with my laughter.

Let me kiss your scars,
and I will bare my own, tentatively perhaps,
but in joy of the salvation each one marks.

Let me kiss your scars,
and we will dance into the night
like lovers and madmen, drunk with life.

Let me kiss your scars.

Betrayal

Yes, I do
know what it is like
to be betrayed.

I am not alone in that.
No.
It is all too common, betrayal

by lovers, by fate,
by people we thought we knew,
but really, never did;

betrayal by time,
by our own weakness,
our own foolishness,
our own blindness.

So yes, I know that pain
and the choices betrayal leaves us.
Do we flee? Do we fight?

Do we build walls,
perfect fortresses to protect our hearts,
fortresses that will too betray us,

and leave us dry, mere husks,
safe, protected,
and empty?

Or do we stand at the gate,
and walk once again into battle,
our hearts open and soft,

in plain view,
foolhardy perhaps,
but vibrant and alive,

knowing love has no death,
except the one
we allow it.

Trusting the Bones

It would be easy to be overwhelmed
as you walk through the old building,
so long neglected,
every square inch a desperate cry
for help, for restoration.

Paint peels.
Molding lies, pulled away from the walls.
Windows are broken.

The floors are scarred
and there is debris, useless

and piled everywhere that needs to be removed
before you begin.

Only the bones remain solid,
and they are invisible,
straight lines of strength
like what remains of your heart,
quiet, strong, determined to stand fast

in the belief that restoration is possible,
even here, where so much seems broken,
you trust the bones, and begin,

The Laws of Restoration

It will take longer than you expect.
It always does.
Destruction and collapse happen in a moment,
but restoration takes time,
each step building on another,

There are no manuals,
No two are the same,
and you will make mistakes.
Sometimes you will have to undo
false steps and the undoing
will anger you, frustrate you,
even make you cry.

It is OK to pause.
Restoration is not a straight line.
Pondering is part of the process,
as is dreaming, imagining, wondering.

Ask advice.
You may believe it is just you alone
in your workshop, but there are others

who have traveled this road,
who have made your mistakes for you,
and will gladly, gladly, share your journey.

And finally, savor the beauty.
Do not wait until it is finished,
for there is beauty in every line and scar,
even in the broken parts.
Especially perhaps, in the broken parts.

No, instead, cherish each small step.
Dream. Imagine, and when you are done
what you have will be more precious
for being loved from the abyss
to a thing of beauty,
obvious to all at the end,
but obvious to you, from the beginning.

My Mother's Poems

My mother died in April. We had to move my father to a nursing
home a couple of months later. And now we have sold the
family home – the only home my sisters remember, and the
place my parents lived since I was ten.

This of course, had meant emptying the home where my
parents lived for 49 years. I have brought four loads of
furniture, books, odds and ends from Virginia to Vermont over
the past three months.
It is odd, seeing things that were always in my parents' home in
my home.

There is both a sense of displacement, and a smile of warm
memories. They are physical reminders of my mother's death
and my dad's decline. But they are also a reminder of things
they instilled in me – the love of old things, the love of the

stories people and things often have, Every time I look at the old post office, or the odd Persian oil lamp that now lives in my dining room, their stories rise unbidden and I smile, and at times, also still cry as their stories flood me with emotion.

One of the strangest things for me have been my mother's poems.

It seems my mother has collected more of my poems than I have. There are hand made books of poems I wrote as a child. There are scribbled poems on envelopes and scraps of paper. There are poems I sent her as parts of letters from college and grad school. There is a hand written book I did, and a bound copy of my grad school thesis, a collection of short stories and poems. There are print outs from my blog going back years.

And, there was one poem she wrote. Just one.

It was a sad thing, that poem. I will not print it here. It was intensely private. None of us knew she had written it. It was one of those finds that often come as you clear out an estate. Something unexpected.

The sadness was not unexpected. In the years since my divorce, my mother had become increasingly open with her frustration and sadness at the last years of her life, how some of her choices had caused her great pain, and kept her back from being all the things she wanted for herself.

Don't get me wrong. She was an amazingly positive woman, right to the end. The people she touched and encouraged is awe inspiring. Months later, I still get notes about the impact she had on peoples' lives. She was an encourager, always an encourager.

But the sadness was there, and her one poem shows how deep it ran.

I wonder at her outlets for that emotion. How did she survive the emotions? I know she talked to my sister. I know she talked to me. But she also held so much in. She often praised me for my "courage" in writing and more than that, posting, my poems each day. "You hang your heart out there." she would say, "Like laundry on the line, where everyone can see the color of your most intimate things.".

We were not raised to do that. Feelings were not encouraged. At least not the expression of them. My father has never understood it. Ultimately he accepted it in me, but never understood what kind of madness makes me write and publish. He believed, with all his heart, that it set me up for being bullied and put down. That feelings are meant to be kept to ourselves.

My Mother understood what I have learned, however. That putting it out there is part of my sanity. It is how I figure things out, wrestling for the words that I often cannot find in discussions or in the midst of what is happening in my life. And I have learned that there's little special about my emotions and struggles and joys except that they are amazingly common. We are more alike than different. And so sharing them, for others who struggle with the words, gives them voice as well as me.

I look at the one poem my mother wrote and never shared. It's good. She was a good writer, a professional and a perfectionist in her wordcraft. But this she wrote this and tucked away. Only to be found now.

I wish she had written more. We carry so much of her in our heart. But we have so little of her in writing. And for me at least, having more words would be powerful, especially if they were as heartfelt as this one poem.

I am grateful for this one poem however. I am grateful that she saved so many of mine – it is like discovering my own journey as a writer. Most of all, I a grateful for her encouragement, which floods back to me as I sort through and read this four inch stack of saved words. I smile. I cry. I smile.

In a way, I realize, all my poems are my mother's poems. And the poems of every person who has touched my heart, in love and pain, or both. That whole stack of scribbled, typed and printed poetry? Hers. And maybe yours. More so than mine.

Be well. Travel wisely.

Tom

Tom Atkins on the web

The Quarry House Website   http://www.quarryhouse.us/

Blog: Poems and photographs
        http://quarryhouse.wordpress.com/

Blog: Art work
        http://theartoftomatkins.wordpress.com/

The Wisdom Cards
        http://thewisdomcards.tumblr.com/

Twitter: tomatkins1955